CONFESSIONS OF GOD OVER US

E C MOSES

CONFESSIONS OF GOD OVER US

E C MOSES

ISBN: 978-1-967375-66-0 (Paperback)
ISBN: 978-1-967375-67-7 (E-book)

Library of Congress Control Number: 2025916443

Printed in the United States of America

Published by:

info@thequippyquill.com
(302) 295-2278

ACKNOWLEDGEMENT

I would like to acknowledge my Lord and Savior, Jesus Christ. It is through Him that I am able to share these words of hope. Philippians 4:6-7 says, "Be anxious for nothing but in everything by prayer and supplication, with thanksgiving, let your requests be made known to God; and the peace of God, which surpasses all understanding, will guard your hearts and minds through Christ Jesus.

INTRODUCTION

Many times, I have wrestled with words spoken over me that were less than kind. Sure, I could go to the Bible and search out scriptures that would reassure me I was not what was being said, but that can be so cumbersome to do. I realized many people experience the same thing in their lives, so I felt led to put together something that could be carried in a person's jacket pocket, or perhaps in a handbag. A small book that could be read repeatedly to retrieve small nuggets of reassurance when times seem overwhelming. In my studies, I have found it true that God is a very good Father and He wants the very best for us. We have been bombarded with negative information that started with our youth. This information has convinced the vast majority that God doesn't care about us or worse, is waiting for us to mess up so He can punish us.

The truths laid out in this book are meant to encourage you and equip you to overcome the negative thoughts and words that come against you. My prayer is that these words bless you and help you overcome the bad in your life.

CHAPTER 1

God's Confession of Love Over Us

God has a lot to say about us. He wrote it down in His Word. He wanted us to know just how much He loves us and desires our complete success in this world during our lifetime. We just need to take the time to find out what He truly said about us.

Because God declared these things about us and over us, we can declare them over our family members and ourselves.

God is a Father. A good father wants the very best for his children. Our heavenly Father is the best. Everything he does is out of love for us. Let's face it, He is love. He tells us to be like Him and walk in love. Look at what He says in 1 John 4:7-8.

> *⁷ Beloved, let us love one another, for love is of God; and everyone who loves is born of God and knows God. ⁸ He who does not love does not know God, for God is love.*

Think about a young couple that has found out they are going to deliver a child into the world. The doctor confirms there will be a child arriving at an approximate date. There is so much excitement in the family. The word goes out about the wonderful news to everyone they know.

The only evidence of a child is knowing that the mother has within her and a lab test that says there is enough of a change in your body chemistry to show she is pregnant. Yet there is joy, excitement, and a genuine love forming for this child that has not been born.

They are loving and preparing for a child by faith. They just know there will be a little one arriving soon, so they do much preparation to allow for the child to become part of their family. There is a room to be decorated with many wonderful things. Purchases of clothing occur, and family members make items, so the little one will have the best attire the young couple can afford.

They spend hours talking about what kind of personality the child will have, what features of themselves the baby will show physically. They speak repeatedly about how wonderful this child will be for the world. How he or she will grow up and accomplish so many things. It is natural for young, expecting parents to spend days and nights talking about their little one who isn't even in their arms, to hear the words.

The mother will often sing songs of love over her coming child that seem to spring up out of her heart. Many will continue to do this after the little one is born. Some fathers will join in, but it seems to be a practice that is performed by mothers more so than by fathers.

These are words and actions of faith. They are preparing this child for greatness with their words. God does the same things. We instinctively do this because we are His children. That is part of our makeup that He put into us.

This is a practice that we have built into us from the Father God above. He rejoices over us; He quiets us when we are frightened, and He sings over us with His love. We find this in Zephaniah 3:16-17.

> *¹⁶ In that day it shall be said to Jerusalem: "Do not fear; Zion, let not your hands be weak. ¹⁷ The Lord your God in your midst, The Mighty One, will save; He will rejoice over you with gladness, He will quiet you with His love, He will rejoice over you with singing."*

From the first words of the Bible, God showed us how to create the surrounding atmosphere. An atmosphere that flourishes and will be full of life. Look at Genesis 1:2-5.

> *² The earth was without form, and void; and darkness was on the face of the deep. And the Spirit of God was hovering over the face of the waters.*
>
> *³ Then God said, "Let there be light" and there was light. ⁴ And God saw the light, that it was good; and God divided the light from the darkness. ⁵ God called the light Day, and the darkness He called Night. So the evening and the morning were the first day.*

God looked at the earth that didn't have any proper form to it and the darkness that was over it. He recognized it was there, but He had something else in mind for the situation. He spoke about what He wanted, and that is exactly what happened.

We instinctively speak words over our lives every day to set in motion what we desire. Unfortunately, if we do not understand and know what God the Father has to say about us, we speak negatively over ourselves. Our fallen nature causes us to speak of the fear that Satan is whispering into our minds.

We must know and believe that God loves us. He gave His only begotten Son for us so that we would have life abundantly with Him. If we look at God through love, we will see all that He has for us. Read 1 John 4:12-16.

> *12 No one has seen God at any time. If we love one another, God abides in us, and His love has been perfected in us. 13 By this we know that we abide in Him, and He in us, because He has given us of His Spirit. 14 And*

> *we have seen and testify that the Father has sent the Son as Savior of the world. 15 Whoever confesses that Jesus is the Son of God, God abides in him, and he in God. 16 And we have known and believed the love that God has for us. God is love, and he who abides in love abides in God, and God in him.*

Because we believe Jesus is the Son of God, He lives in us. He reveals the love of the Father to us every day. Since He is in the Father and the Father is in Him, the Father is also in us. That wonderful love is in us because both the Father and Jesus are in us.

To help you understand this concept, think about a person who has a great deal of positive influence in your life. Perhaps it is one of your parents, or a grandparent. Have you ever noticed that when you are pondering about something that is troubling you, you seem to hear their voice in your head telling you what to do?

If we will yield to that voice of God that we hear on the inside of us, allow His love to guide us in what we say and do, He will cause us to be a blessing to everyone in our sphere of influence.

When He walked the earth, Jesus declared the Father to the people. He is still declaring the Father to us now. They hope to walk every waking moment with us. John 17:24-26 states the following.

> *24 "Father, I desire that they also whom You gave Me may be with Me where I am, that they may behold My glory which You have given Me; for You loved Me before the foundation of the world. 25 O righteous Father! The world has not known You, but I have known You; and these have known that You sent Me. 26 And I have declared to them Your name, and will declare it, that the love with which You loved Me may be in them, and I in them."*

God is love. He is a love that surpasses anything that we can comprehend. His love is all-encompassing, and so deep that we find it difficult to put it into words that properly describe it. Here is what the Bible says about love in 1 Corinthians 13:4-8a.

> *4 Love suffers long and is kind; love does not envy; love does not parade itself, is not puffed up; 5 does not behave rudely, does not seek its own, is not provoked, thinks no evil; 6 does not rejoice in iniquity, but rejoices in the truth; 7 bears all things, believes all things, hopes all things, endures all things.*
>
> *8 Love never fails.*

We can declare that because we have received THE LOVE and because we have believed THE LOVE, we can confidently state we will practice and walk in love and be a walking example to everyone around us. HE IS LOVE!

We are born of His love. He gave of Himself so we could be free to love Him in return. Read what God said in Ephesians 5:1-2.

> *5Therefore be imitators of God as dear children. 2And walk in love, as Christ also has loved us and given Himself for us, an offering and a sacrifice to God for a sweet-smelling aroma.*

God's love instills great joy in our hearts. That joy gives us strength to accomplish many great things. We find that strength in Nehemiah 8:10.

> *10 Then he said to them, "Go your way, eat the fat, drink the sweet, and send portions to those for whom nothing is prepared; for this day is holy to our Lord. Do not sorrow, for the joy of the Lord is your strength."*

The love of God gives us peace that the world does not understand. It is difficult for people to be in the middle of adversity and be at peace. It is God's love that brings that peace to our souls. Here are 2 examples of the peace that Jesus gives to us.

John 14:27.

> *27 Peace I leave with you, My peace I give to you; not as the world gives do I give to you. Let not your heart be troubled, neither let it be afraid.*

Philippians 4:6-7.

> *6 Be anxious for nothing, but in everything by prayer and supplication, with thanksgiving, let*

your requests be made known to God; ⁷ and the peace of God, which surpasses all understanding, will guard your hearts and minds through Christ Jesus.

In the natural, we may go through some form of training to prepare us for a new position at work, or perhaps to develop a new physical skill. At the time we are going through learning these skills and struggling both mentally and physically, we certainly do not enjoy the difficulties. It is important that we understand that God's love for us keeps us as we go through similar trials to build our faith.

His love for us produces patience in our character, making us perfect and complete.

James 1:2-4.

² My brethren, count it all joy when you fall into various trials, ³knowing that the testing of your faith produces patience. ⁴ But let patience have its perfect work, that you may be perfect and complete, lacking nothing.

His love in us makes us gentle and kind, not proud and boastful.

1 Corinthians 13:4.

> *⁴ Love suffers long and is kind; love does not envy; love does not parade itself, is not puffed up;*

His love puts His light in us, and His goodness, righteousness, and truth are working in us.

Ephesians 5:8-10.

> *⁸ For you were once darkness, but now you are light in the Lord. Walk as children of light ⁹ (for the fruit of the Spirit is in all goodness, righteousness, and truth), ¹⁰ finding out what is acceptable to the Lord.*

God's love working in us leads us to be faithful in all that we do.

Proverbs 28:20.

> *²⁰A faithful man will abound with blessings, But he who hastens to be rich will not go unpunished.*

God is our Father, and His instructions, out of love, lead us to life.

Proverbs 4:20-23.

[20] *My son, give attention to my words; Incline your ear to my sayings.* [21] *Do not let them depart from your eyes; Keep them in the midst of your heart;* [22] *For they are life to those who find them, And health to all their flesh.* [23] *Keep your heart with all diligence, For out of it spring the issues of life.*

CHAPTER 2

God's Confession of Prosperity Over Us

Review and study these scriptures to see just a few of the things that He wants to do for you. He did not mean you to be poor but rich in goods so that you can bless others.

No matter how much you love God, you may limit what He can do in your life by believing—maybe even somewhere deep down—that His goodness doesn't apply to you, at least not in *every* situation. You can change that!

These verses (and there are many, many more than what is here) support the truth that God neither wants His children to be afraid of money, nor does He want them to obsess over it. Money is a tool, neither good nor bad. Much like a contractor would need a hammer, a drill, or a crane to build a physical house; we all require money to build our financial houses. And like any other resource at our disposal, it belongs to

Him. We don't truly own it. Instead, we are called to be "stewards" of it (Luke 16).

Jesus told a parable, a story to show an example, of an unjust steward in Luke 16:1-13 (NASB).

> *16 Now He was also saying to the disciples, "There was a rich man who had a manager, and this manager was reported to him as squandering his possessions. 2 And he summoned him and said to him, 'What is this I hear about you? Give an accounting of your management, for you can no longer be manager.' 3 And the manager said to himself, 'What am I to do, since my master is taking the management away from me? I am not strong enough to dig; I am ashamed to beg. 4 I know what I will do, so that when I am removed from the management people will welcome me into their homes.' 5 And he summoned each one of his master's debtors, and he began saying to the first, 'How much do you owe my master?' 6 And he said, 'A*

hundred jugs of oil.' And he said to him, 'Take your bill, and sit down quickly and write fifty.' ⁷ *Then he said to another, 'And how much do you owe?' And he said, 'A hundred kors of wheat.' He *said to him, 'Take your bill, and write eighty.'* ⁸ *And his master complimented the unrighteous manager because he had acted shrewdly; for the sons of this age are more shrewd in relation to their own kind than the sons of light.* ⁹ *And I say to you, make friends for yourselves by means of the wealth of unrighteousness, so that when it is all gone, they will receive you into the eternal dwellings.*

¹⁰ *"The one who is faithful in a very little thing is also faithful in much; and the one who is unrighteous in a very little thing is also unrighteous in much.* ¹¹ *Therefore, if you have not been faithful in the use of unrighteous wealth, who will entrust the true wealth to you?* ¹² *And if you have not been faithful in the use of that which is another's, who will give you that*

> which is your own? *¹³ No servant can serve two masters; for either he will hate the one and love the other, or he will be devoted to one and despise the other. You cannot serve God and wealth."*

In this story, Jesus explained that the unrighteous people in this world are better at managing their wealth than we, the righteous people that follow Him. We have been told that money is evil, and we are not to have any of it because it will have us. The money, or wealth, is not evil. It is merely a tool that we should use to further the kingdom of God on the earth.

By keeping our focus on God and allowing His love to guide us and teach us how to manage, or steward, the finances, He will continue to give us more and more of it.

These are His words over you so you can stand confidently and speak them over yourself. Personalize each scripture so that when you read it out loud, you are saying it about you.

Psalm 35:27 God wants me to prosper so that He can be magnified.

> *²⁷Let them shout for joy and be glad, who favor my righteous cause; and let them say continually, "Let the Lord be magnified, who has pleasure in the prosperity of His servant."*

Proverbs 10:22 The Lord takes delight in blessing me and wants me to be happy in it.

> *²²The blessing of the Lord makes one rich, and He adds no sorrow with it.*

Deuteronomy 8:18 God enables me to get wealth because He wants to show His covenant to me.

> *¹⁸And you shall remember the Lord your God, for it is He who gives you power to get wealth, that He may establish His covenant which He swore to your fathers, as it is this day.*

2 Corinthians 8:9 He came to earth to show us how to become rich.

> *⁹For you know the grace of our Lord Jesus Christ, that though He was rich, yet for your sakes He became*

> *poor, that you through His poverty might become rich.*

John 10:10 Jesus came to give us life more abundantly

> *10The thief does not come except to steal, and to kill, and to destroy. I have come that they may have life, and that they may have it more abundantly.*

Philippians 4:19 God is rich beyond measure and desires for us to be rich as well.

> *19And my God shall supply all your need according to His riches in glory by Christ Jesus.*

1 John 4:17 He is walking in Righteousness, Health and Wealth, so should we right now.

> *17Love has been perfected among us in this: that we may have boldness in the day of judgment; because as He is, so are we in this world.*

Psalm 84:11 The Lord will not withhold any good thing from me.

> *11For the Lord God is a sun and shield; the Lord will give grace and glory; no good thing will He withhold from those who walk uprightly.*

Galatians 3:13,14 I am redeemed from the curse of the law and The BLESSING is on Me!

> *13Christ has redeemed us from the curse of the law, having become a curse for us (for it is written, "Cursed is everyone who hangs on a tree"), 14that the blessing of Abraham might come upon the Gentiles in Christ Jesus, that we might receive the promise of the Spirit through faith.*

Psalm 25:12-13 The one who reverences the LORD will live in prosperity.

> *12 Who is the man that fears the Lord? Him shall He teach in the way He chooses. 13He himself shall dwell in prosperity, and his descendants shall inherit the earth.*

Proverbs 3:13-18 The wisdom of the LORD brings long life, riches, and honor.

> *13 Happy is the man who finds wisdom, and the man who gains understanding; 14 For her proceeds are better than the profits of silver, and her gain than fine gold. 15 She is more precious than rubies, and all the things you may desire cannot compare with her. 16 Length of days is in her right hand. In her left hand, riches and honor. 17 Her ways are ways of pleasantness, and all her paths are peace. 18 She is a tree of life to those who take hold of her, and happy are all who retain her.*

Deuteronomy 28:1–14 Because I am diligent to obey the voice of the Lord, His BLESSING is overtaking me!

> *1 "Now it shall come to pass, if you diligently obey the voice of the Lord your God, to observe carefully all His commandments which I command you today, that the Lord your God will set you high above all nations of the earth.*

²And all these blessings shall come upon you and overtake you, because you obey the voice of the Lord your God:

³"Blessed shall you be in the city, and blessed shall you be in the country.

⁴"Blessed shall be the fruit of your body, the produce of your ground and the increase of your herds, the increase of your cattle and the offspring of your flocks.

⁵"Blessed shall be your basket and your kneading bowl.

⁶"Blessed shall you be when you come in, and blessed shall you be when you go out.

⁷"The Lord will cause your enemies who rise against you to be defeated before your face; they shall come out against you one way and flee before you seven ways.

⁸"The Lord will command the blessing on you in your storehouses and in all to which you set your hand, and He will bless you in the land which the Lord your God is giving you.

9 "The Lord will establish you as a holy people to Himself, just as He has sworn to you, if you keep the commandments of the Lord your God and walk in His ways.

10 Then all peoples of the earth shall see that you are called by the name of the Lord, and they shall be afraid of you.

11 And the Lord will grant you plenty of goods, in the fruit of your body, in the increase of your livestock, and in the produce of your ground, in the land of which the Lord swore to your fathers to give you.

12 The Lord will open to you His good treasure, the heavens, to give the rain to your land in its season, and to bless all the work of your hand. You shall lend to many nations, but you shall not borrow.

13 And the Lord will make you the head and not the tail; you shall be above only, and not be beneath, if you heed the commandments of the Lord your God, which I command you today, and are careful to observe them.

14 So you shall not turn aside from any of the words which I command you this day, to the right or the left, to go after other gods to serve them.

CHAPTER 3

God's Confession of Health and Healing Over Us

God wants you to be healthy, free of disease and sickness.

The LORD GOD pursues us while we are yet sinners. He forgives us of our sins and then heals us. In prayer one day, I asked why, and He said, "The heart must be prepared to receive." We cannot receive God's goodness until our hearts have received forgiveness. The guilt of sin stands in the way of our redemption, so the Lord forgives us, breaks the fallow ground of our hearts, and softens the soil so that His love can penetrate and redeem us.

2 Chronicles 30:18-20 demonstrates this. Hezekiah prayed for the people, saying, The good LORD pardon every one that prepares his heart to seek and follow God, the LORD GOD. The LORD, the self-existent I AM, hearkened to Hezekiah and healed the

people. God did what Hezekiah asked of Him.

Jesus did the same thing while He was here on earth. In Mark 2:1-12, a paralyzed man was brought before Jesus. They lowered him through the roof to get him in front of Jesus. Jesus saw the faith of the four men and turned to the paralyzed man and said, "Son, your sins are forgiven." He wasn't healed just yet, but this prepared the man's heart to receive the healing that Jesus was about to pronounce on him.

Jesus showed His power to forgive sins and heal the broken body. After rebuking the scribes that were sitting there, He said to the paralyzed man, "I say to you, arise, take up your bed, and go to your house." Immediately, the man got up and did exactly what Jesus told him to do.

Healing starts with the heart. First, we receive His love and forgiveness. Then we can receive His healing power into our bodies and walk completely healed and whole.

Meditate on these scriptures until they become so real to you, no matter what sickness is going on around you, it cannot come on you.

Exodus 15:26 I am the Lord that heals you.

> *26He said, "If you listen carefully to the Lord your God and do what is right in his eyes, if you pay attention to his commands and keep all his decrees, I will not bring on you any of the diseases I brought on the Egyptians, for **I am the Lord, who heals you**."*

Exodus 23:25-26 The Lord will give **me** a full lifespan.

> *25Worship the Lord your God, and his blessing will be on your food and water. I will take away sickness from among you, and none will miscarry or be barren in your land. **I will give you a full life span**.*

Deuteronomy 7:14-15 The Lord will keep **me** free from **every** disease.

*¹⁴You will be blessed more than any other people; none of your men or women will be childless, nor will any of your livestock be without young. **The Lord will keep you free from every disease**. He will not inflict on you the horrible diseases you knew in Egypt, but he will inflict them on all who hate you.*

Deuteronomy 30:19-20 Choose Life.

*¹⁹This day I call the heavens and the earth as witnesses against you that I have set before you life and death, blessings and curses. **Now choose life**, so that you and your children may live and that you may love the Lord your God, listen to his voice, and hold fast to him. For the Lord is your life, and he will give you many years in the land he swore to give to your fathers, Abraham, Isaac and Jacob.*

1 Kings 8:56 Not one word has failed of ALL the good promises He gave **me**.

*56"Praise be to the Lord, who has given rest to his people Israel just as he promised. **Not one word has failed of all the good promises he gave** through his servant Moses."*

Psalm 91:9-10 I will make the Lord my refuge and no harm will overtake **me**.

9If you say, "The Lord is my refuge," and you make the Most High your dwelling, no harm will overtake you, no disaster will come near your tent.

Psalm 91:14-16 I will love the Lord and He will satisfy **me** with long life.

*14"**Because he loves me," says the Lord**, "I will rescue him; I will protect him, for he acknowledges my name. He will call on me, and I will answer him; I will be with him in trouble, I will deliver him and honor him. **With long life I will satisfy him** and show him my salvation."*

Psalm 103:1-5 Praise the Lord who heals all **my** diseases.

> *¹Praise the Lord, my soul; all my inmost being, praise his holy name. Praise the Lord, my soul, and forget not all his benefits — **who** forgives all your sins and **heals all your diseases**, who redeems your life from the pit and crowns you with love and compassion, who satisfies your desires with good things so that your youth is renewed like the eagle's.*

Psalm 107:19-21 The Lord sent His word and healed **me**.

> *¹⁹Then they cried to the Lord in their trouble, and he saved them from their distress. **He sent out his word and healed them**; he rescued them from the grave. Let them give thanks to the Lord for his unfailing love and his wonderful deeds for mankind.*

Psalm 118:17 **I** will not die, but live.

> *¹⁷I will not die but live, and will proclaim what the Lord has done.*

Proverbs 4:20-24 I will keep your words in **my** heart for they are life.

*²⁰My son, **pay attention to what I say**; turn your ear to **my words**. Do not let them out of your sight, keep them within your heart; for they **are life** to those who find them and health to one's whole body. Above all else, guard your heart, for everything you do flows from it. Keep your mouth free of perversity; keep corrupt talk far from your lips.*

Matthew 8:2-3 Jesus is willing to heal **me**.

*²A man with leprosy came and knelt before him and said, "Lord, if you are willing, you can make me clean." Jesus reached out his hand and touched the man. **"I am willing,"** he said. "Be clean!" Immediately, he was cleansed of his leprosy.*

Matthew 8:16-17 Jesus, by His word, healed **all** the sick.

*¹⁶When evening came, many who were demon-possessed were brought to him, and he drove out the spirits **with a word** and healed **all** the* *sick. This was to fulfill what was spoken through the prophet Isaiah: "He took up our infirmities and bore our diseases."*

Matthew 15:30-31 I will kneel at Jesus' feet and He will heal me.

30Great crowds came to him, bringing the lame, the blind, the crippled, the mute, and many others, and laid them at his feet; and he healed them. The people were amazed when they saw the mute speaking, the crippled made well, the lame walking and the blind seeing. And they praised the God of Israel.

Matthew 18:18-19 I will bind evil and loose the Blessing of the Lord.

18 "Truly I tell you, whatever you bind on earth will be bound in heaven, and whatever you loose on earth will be loosed in heaven. "Again, truly I tell you that if two of you on earth agree about anything they ask for, it will be done for them by my Father in heaven.

Matthew 21:21-22 **I** will believe and receive whatever **I** ask for.

> *[21] Jesus replied, "Truly I tell you, if you have faith and do not doubt, not only can you do what was done to the fig tree, but also you can say to this mountain, 'Go, throw yourself into the sea,' and it will be done. If you believe, you will receive whatever you ask for in prayer."*

Mark 9:23 Everything is possible for me because **I believe**.

> *[23] "'If you can'?" said Jesus. **"Everything is possible for one who believes**."*

Mark 10:27 Everything is possible with God.

> *[27] Jesus looked at them and said, "With man this is impossible, but not with God; **all things are possible with God**."*

Mark 11:22-24 **I** will have what **I** say.

> *[22] "Have faith in God," Jesus answered. "Truly I tell you, **if anyone says** to*

*this mountain, 'Go, throw yourself
into the sea,' **and does not doubt**
in their heart but believes that what
they say will happen, **it will be
done for them**. Therefore, I tell you,
whatever you ask for in prayer,
believe that you have received it, and
it will be yours.*

Mark 16:14-18 In Jesus name, **I** will
drive out demons and heal the sick.

*[14]Later Jesus appeared to the Eleven
as they were eating; he rebuked them
for their lack of faith and their
stubborn refusal to believe those who
had seen him after he had risen. He
said to them, "Go into all the world
and preach the gospel to all creation.
Whoever believes and is baptized will
be saved, but whoever does not
believe will be condemned. And these
signs will accompany those who
believe: **In my name they will
drive out demons;** they will speak
in new tongues; they will pick up
snakes with their hands; and when
they drink deadly poison, it will not*

*hurt them at all; **they will place their hands on sick people, and they will get well.***"

Luke 6:19 Power comes from Jesus and heals **me**.

¹⁹and the people all tried to touch him, because power was coming from him and healing them all.

Luke 9:23 **I** will go out and heal the sick.

²³and he sent them out to proclaim the kingdom of God and to heal the sick.

I can't imagine doing these things by our own strength. Without the strength of God's love operating inside us, we can do nothing. Here are some scriptures that speak to God's strength that He made available to us.

My spirit is built up strong in the Lord.

Psalm 22:19.

¹⁹ But You, O Lord, do not be far from Me; O My Strength, hasten to help Me!

Jesus is my strength!

Psalm 20:6.

> *⁶ Now I know that the Lord saves His anointed; He will answer him from His holy heaven with the saving strength of His right hand.*

I will go in the strength of the LORD.

Psalm 71:16.

> *¹⁶ I will go in the strength of the Lord God; I will make mention of Your righteousness, of Yours only.*

My love is for my LORD who has armed me with strength.

Psalm 18:39.

> *³⁹ For You have armed me with strength for the battle; You have subdued under me those who rose up against me.*

I am blessed because I found my strength in You, LORD, and I go from strength to strength.

Psalm 84:5,7.

⁵ Blessed is the man whose strength is in You, whose heart is set on pilgrimage.

⁷ They go from strength to strength; Each one appears before God in Zion.

My confidence and strength keep my heart at peace, for it comes from You, Oh LORD.

Psalm 27:3.

³ Though an army may encamp against me, My heart shall not fear; Though war may rise against me, In this I will be confident.

LORD, You are my strength, and my shield. I will sing to You, Oh LORD.

Psalm 28:7.

⁷ The Lord is my strength and my shield; My heart trusted in Him, and I am helped; Therefore, my heart greatly rejoices, and with my song I will praise Him.

Using the substance of these verses, pray this prayer with all of your heart!

I believe I receive my spirit built up, strong. Jesus is my strength! I will go in the strength of The LORD.

I love You, O LORD, my strength. You have girded me with strength. Therefore, I go from strength to strength.

I am strong in The LORD. He is my life, of whom shall I be afraid? LORD, You are my strength and my shield!

ABOUT THE AUTHOR

E C Moses grew up believing that God was against him. Years of abuse and isolation led to uncovering the truth, and he discovered a deeper understanding of God that led to the creation of his 1st book, *Man Has Put God on Trial and Found Him Guilty*. He recently wrestled with words spoken over him that were less than kind then he realized many people experience the same thing in their lives. After a period of studying, he has found the truth that God is a very good Father. His desire to share the truth led to the creation of this book. E C Moses holds a Doctorate of Ministry and actively teaches seminary-level courses, helping students gain a true understanding of the Bible's message.

www.ingramcontent.com/pod-product-compliance
Lightning Source LLC
Chambersburg PA
CBHW031238120626
46545CB00003B/1183

* 9 7 8 1 9 6 7 3 7 5 6 6 0 *